To My Forever Love

To My Forever Love

100 Affirmations of Love and Appreciation

by

Ann Marie Jackson

TO MY FOREVER LOVE
Ann Marie Jackson

Paper back Book - ISBN: 978-1-7772126-5-0
Ebook Book -ISBN: 978-1-7772126-6-7

INTRODUCTION

Hello my Love, it is me, "LOVE". You prayed for me and I manifested right before your very eyes in the flesh. You are pleasing to my eyes. You had no idea that God and his angels were preparing me for you and you for me. Patience was key to our union. We needed to heal our wounded past individually, so collectively we can be a force to be reckoned with.

The road has not been easy. I cried a few tears on my journey to finding you only because you promised that you would find me, yet the road seemed endless. I felt hunger and thirst for you as you felt for me. The promises we made to each other still remain. I've had time to think of all the words I want to express to you once you come home. I am ready to be your peace. It is time to rest My Forever Love.

About the Author

Ann Marie Jackson is an International Relationship Coach, Master Matchmaker, Author and self-described" Divine Feminine". As a woman of stature and all woman, Ms. Jackson's experiences have been experiential, God-inspired and evolutionary. Her unique approach to empowering her client's focuses on getting them to understand the real meaning of love for their better lives. She has more than 20 years of experience counseling and coaching individuals who were in, between or out of dysfunctional relationships. Her first of four forthcoming books, **"Love: Sacred as an Orgasm,"** Finding **genuine love** in an **over sexualized society"**, provides practical strategies to establish and maintain healthy relationships and how to safely extinguish toxic ones. Through her school, Connect Me Academy, Ms. Jackson will further promote healthy relationships that endure the test of time and trial through her workbooks, workshops, online courses, seminars, webinars, and retreats. As she refines her message of healing to individuals, couples and their families, her approach will evolve according to constructive feedback from her clients. The growth and development of client feedback and testimonies will constantly be reflected in new, improved, and repaired relationships. The divine guidance of God and the collective wisdom Ms. Jackson will gain on this journey will strip lies and masks from the unhappy and nonproductive nature that seems to characterize many of today's relationships. As the messenger, Ms. Jackson only requires that anyone embrace the concepts in her book, academy and associated enterprises as the validation to a healthier and longer life and relationships.

DEDICATION

This book is dedicated to every wounded broken man or woman who has loved and lost, over and over again. It is time to heal your past traumas and start a new journey of loving you. In doing so, you will learn how to give and receive love openly, honestly, and freely without the thought of being hurt again.

When a relationship does not work, it simply means that your healing is not complete. You have to revisit some issues in your life and deal with them head-on. These issues can stem from mommy, daddy trauma, neglect, abandonment issues, childhood trauma including molestation, etcetera.

The only way to love is "Freely". If you are holding back on love, meaning only giving fifty percent of yourself to your partner instead of one hundred percent, then remain single and work on your self-love. Self-love is the most rewarding love you will ever receive from any relationship. Be the love you want to attract.

TO MY FOREVER LOVE!

100 Affirmations Of Love And Appreciation

Our love and Union will never die to divorce. I live in you and you in me.

I PROMISE

1

You will never have to worry about me cheating. If I cheat with another, I cheat myself, cause I am you and it will hurt me to the core as it will you.

2

We will communicate well, because
I want you all over my innermost thoughts
and feelings when it comes to us.

3

I thank God that you are healthy, strong and capable of loving me through the storms of life

4

I will always love you like I love myself, "unconditionally".

5

I saved myself for you because
I knew you were expecting me.

6

I got married twice having you in mind.
I attracted men physically,
but my spiritual eyes needed to be
awakened for us.

7

Our past relationships were painful, and breakups were meant to help us find each other. I realize that there are no good or bad relationships, only classes designed to wake us and discover our self.

8

---

*Our children will love that we are together.
We will teach them about true love by
our example*

9

We will be the perfect example of love to our friends, family, and our community

10

I will respect you as my King;
I am your Queen

11

We will experience intimacy in and out of the bedroom with your words, your stare, your touch, your gifts, your presence, and just always being there for me

12

I will apologize to you when I am wrong

13

I will cook for you, feed you nutritious foods, as we manifest together our vision, goals and purpose united as one

14

No one has ever made me feel
the way that you do.

15

I will protect your heart at all times,
as you have protected mine.

16

Other men have nothing on you.

17

Our friendship means the world to me

18

---

*We were chosen for each other
by the creator.*

19

*You are exactly what I dreamed of
as a little girl, and so much more*

20

I love your handsome face, soft hand that caresses me daily, your beautiful smile, while looking at me, simply fills me up.

21

Your kisses let me know everything you're thinking, wanting, and feeling for me.

22

Your stature says "King"

23

---

*I will be your sounding board when
you arrive home from being beaten
up by the world*

24

You brilliant mind drives me crazy

25

Your shoe size fits per-fect-ly

26

I am your happily ever after

27

I love the way you speak to our children

28

I love the way you forgave your mom for your childhood trauma. I love that you gave her a second chance to be in your life. Not for her, but for us.

29

I thank you for forgiving you dad for not being there when you needed him the most. He missed out on raising an amazing King.

30

---

*Thank you for forgiving your past,
because without doing so, our future
could be uncertain*

31

---

*Thank you for Setting boundaries
with friends and family for the success
of our union*

32

Thank you for listening to my dreams
goals and desires

33

Thank you for the brand new Mercedes Benz. You listened.

34

Thank you for the home in the
country, you listened.

35

---

*Thank you for the three weeks getaway
to the Caribbean. You listened*

36

I love spending time with you.
It is priceless

37

I love the way you love me

38

I love the way you care for me

39

I admire how attentive you are

40

I love the way you touch my face with your soft manicured hands as your eyes penetrated into mine

41

---

*I appreciate the way you clean me up
when you take the bugger from my eyes.
Thank you*

42

You are perfect in every way.

43

I choose you

44

You are the reason I smile when I am driving down the freeway

45

You are the reason I speak life into others

46

You are the reason I want to come home everyday

47

You are the reason I succeed on so many levels

48

---

*You are the reason I am the best
mother to our children*

49

*You are the reason I have beautiful
dreams at night*

50

You are the reason I waited

51

*You are the reason I have everything
I could ever dreamed for*

52

You are the one I see in my dreams

53

I am so happy we found each other

54

Thank you for making peace with your exes. Recognizing that they were the teachers you choose to teach you self-love. You needed to love you first before you could love me. That was the lesson. Thank them instead of hating.

55

Thank you for creating peace with your siblings. You did it for us. Even though you're not close with them, I understand. We have each other now, to eternity.

56

Thank you for sitting with God in silence daily.

57

Thank you for taking the time to bless the food before we partake

58

I love it when you thank God for me

59

---

*I love it when you speak to
our children in love*

60

I love the way you make incredible love to me

61

I love the way you plan our nights together

62

You have such great taste in music

63

I love the way you surprise me by coming home early to cook me dinner

64

Thank you for being the King of our castle

65

---

*I appreciate the way you help
with the chores*

66

I appreciate the way you pay attention to details with the laundry, separating the white from colors

67

You are such a great cook

68

Thank you for taking out the garbage
without me asking King.

69

---

*I appreciate you doing the dishes
when necessary*

70

Thank you for making the bed when you have some extra time in the morning

71

Thank you for remembering to put the toilet seat down so I don't fall in

72

Thank you for putting my needs
ahead of your own

73

---

*Thank you for understanding that
I really do have a headache, and all
I truly need from you is to cuddle*

74

---

*Thank you for helping me understand
the things you enjoy so that I can enjoy
them with you*

75

---

*I will always support you with your
dreams and vision*

76

I will let you lead

77

I honor and respect who you are

78

God took his time when he created you for me

79

I forgive you for not waiting for me

80

I forgive you for having our children with another woman, as you have forgiven me for having our children with another man

81

I am in love with your past present and future. You are now better for us.

82

Your pain is now my pain.
We are in this together

83

I look forward to becoming very
old with you

84

Our sex life will always be spicy. In the car, at the function, just touch me

85

We will explore this earth together like no one else exist but us

86

Our family will never be broken, we will be an example of true love

87

---

*Thank you for having accountable friends
who can lift you up when you're down
and speak life into you*

88

I am appreciative that we respect each other's boundaries

89

Thank you for scheduling time to talk when we have a disagreement

90

Thank you for clearing your schedule to spend quality time together

91

Thank you for putting our family first

92

Thank you for serving me so unselfishly.
I will continue to reciprocate your love.

93

Thank you for understanding that I don't have a relationship with my siblings and not judging me for it.

94

I have given up my BOSS status for you

95

I have done the work of healing
my past for us to win, and I know
you've done the same

96

Submitting to your will for us will never be a problem in our household

97

---

*I am no longer single and available
to other suitors*

98

I don't need a fifty, fifty love with you. It's 100 percent with you babe. I'm all in

99

You occupy my whole heart

100

---

*Our love language is loving
communication, honesty and forgiveness*

These Loving Affirmations will help you determine whether or not you have done the work of healing and forgiving past trauma from childhood to present, where you are now ready to give and receive love freely.

It is imperative to find peace with your past from exes, parents, siblings, friendships and most importantly yourself. Forgiveness is the key to your healing. When you forgive your past, you are now free to love openly and selfless.

By forgiving your past hurt and trauma, you are now free to entertain healthier relationships.

You will have access to a second chance at love. Be sure to pick up a copy of my book, "BORN AGAIN SELF", A Second Chance To Fly Higher. Through forgiveness, you are able to give one hundred percent of yourself in love to a deserving partner without the fear of being hurt.

Now that you've done the work of healing, write your words of affirmation to your new person. With these affirmations, you can hold each other accountable as your journey together may experiences major or minor bumps along this beautiful path to reclaim amazing love.